iets anders | something else

iets anders
vertaling van gedichten | translation of poems
something else

ingmar heytze & saskia stehouwer

by Joel Thomas Katz and Robert Perry

DUTCH POET PRESS

Copyright 2017 © Dutch Poet Press
Robert Perry and Joel Thomas Katz
All Rights Reserved.

ISBN: 978-0-9967056-1-5

For the poems in Dutch:

Copyright 2017 © Ingmar Heytze
and Uitgeverij Podium BV

Copyright 2014 © Saskia Stehouwer
and Uitgeverij Marmer BV

Dutch Poet Press
Palo Alto, California
dutchpoetpress.com

For Penny and Jessica

Acknowledgments

We thank these people for the invaluable contribution they made to the publication of this book. Above all, we extend our *hartelijkste bedankt* to the poets **Ingmar Heytze** and **Saskia Stehouwer** for their extraordinary poetry and their gracious generosity in allowing us to translate and publish their work and for offering such wonderful advice.

++++

Peter Prins of Stichting Perdu, the all-poetry bookshop in Amsterdam, who started it all by suggesting to Joel "you might find that these two books by Ingmar Heytze and Saskia Stehouwer would be very interesting to translate."

Uitgeverij Podium (Amsterdam) who graciously allowed us to reprint the original Dutch poems from two Ingmar Heytze books: *Utrecht voor beginners & gevorderden : verzamelde Utrechtse gedichten* (Utrecht for beginners & the advanced : collected Utrecht poems, 2015), and *Voor de liefste onbekende: bijna alle gedichten* (For the most beloved unknown: almost all the poems, 2016).

Uitgeverij Marmer (Baarn) who graciously allowed us to reprint the original Dutch poems from Saskia Stehouwer's book *Wachtkamers: gedichten* (Waiting rooms: poems, 2014).

Karen Kao, the novelist Joel met at the Napa Valley Writers Conference in July 2016 who generously offered her comments and corrections for our translations, providing useful insights into the Dutch language.

Palo Alto Café with Keyvan "Kevin" Alikermanshahi and the congenial staff where our translations and fruitful discussions took place.

Catamaran Literary Reader for publishing our translation of Saskia's "Stappen in de straat" (Footsteps in the street).

The Massachusetts Review for publishing our translation of Ingmar's "Vos onder ijs" (Fox under ice).

Dutch Studies Program, University of California at Berkeley, who years ago provided co-translator Robert Perry with instruction in the Dutch language and a formidable introduction to Dutch art and culture that ignited his interest in Dutch poetry.

Familie Franken, the Dutch cousins of co-translator Robert Perry, beginning with his first cousin Elsie Franken-Holt along with her husband Fric and the rest of the family to whom Robert is forever grateful for his full and direct and intimate experience of the Netherlands.

Photo Credits

Ingmar Heytze and Utrecht's Domtoren **(Cathedral Tower)** by Chris Heijmans (chrisheijmans.nl) with permission of the photographer.

Map of Utrecht (1870) drawn by J. Kuijper.

Het Beste en de rest designed by Borinka and published by Uitgeverij Podium, 2008. Photo by Alice Day.

Ingmar as a child provided by the poet and taken by a family member.

Letters van Utrecht by Elise Roders (elise.roders.info) with permission of the photographer.

++++

Saskia Stehouwer as an adult by Rosa van Ederen (rosavanederen.nl) with permission of the photographer.

Saskia as a child | Beach at Zandvoort & Vlieland | Saskia's giraffe tattoo provided by the poet.

Wachtkamers designed by Riesenkind with illustration by Noor Agter and published by Uitgeverij Marmer, 2014. Photo by Alice Day.

Contents

Introduction

+++

1 Gedichten | Poems

3 INGMAR HEYTZE
  6 Vos onder ijs
  7 Fox under ice

  8 Voor de liefste onbekende
  9 For the most beloved unknown

  10 Bericht aan de reizigers
  11 Attention travelers

  14 Aan de bruid
  15 To the bride

  16 Wij zorgen ervor
  17 We'll take care of it

  18 Utrecht 2001
  19 Utrecht 2001

  20 160
  21 160

  22 Utrecht voor beginners
  23 Utrecht for beginners

  24 Stadsdichten
  25 City poetry

27 SASKIA STEHOUWER

30 Het onvermogen van de voorbijganger
31 The inability of the passerby

32 Bezoek
33 Visit

34 Twee kantjes
35 Two sides

38 Huismeester
39 Caretaker

40 Nu
41 Now

42 Voor
43 For

44 Wij sturen niemand naar bed
45 We send no one to bed

46 Schifting
47 Sifting

48 Stappen in de straat
49 Footsteps in the street

+++

Essays

53 So much depends upon ... a Dutch Poet
by Robert Perry

69 The *iets anders* | *something else* of Language
by Joel Thomas Katz

87 Translation Notes

Introduction

The project for this book began on a visit to Amsterdam where poet-translator Joel Katz found his way to *Perdu*, a poetry bookstore on the Kloveniersburgwal near the center of the city. There he asked the kind and attentive Peter Prins for two books by contemporary poets that Joel could take home to translate into English.

Joel followed the proprietor through the shop and was handed two slim volumes of poems by very different poets, *Het Beste en de rest* (Uitgeverij Podium, 2006) by Ingmar Heytze and *Wachtkamers* (Uitgeverij Marmer, 2014) by Saskia Stehouwer.

Equipped with several months of listening to *Learn Dutch* CDs produced by Pimsleur Language Programs, a very determined Joel began his endeavor of translating a selection of poems from each volume, initially with the help of a Dutch native living in Palo Alto.

Joel brought the books to share with Robert Perry, who had a table at a local book arts fair where Robert presented his newly established imprint, Dutch Poet Press. He is a graphic designer, book artist, and poet who has belonged to the same poetry group as Joel for many years.

A month or two later, Robert offered to brush off his Dutch and help Joel with his ambitious undertaking. Specializing in Dutch art and architecture as a student of art history, Robert has long been interested in the art and culture of the Netherlands with poetry as a particular passion of his.

Joel and Robert met faithfully nearly every week for over a year at the Palo Alto Café where they applied themselves to the enjoyable task of translation. They let the process flow naturally without a thought about timing or publishing, even though it struck Robert that this would be an ideal book for his Dutch Poet Press. Nonetheless Robert chose to follow Joel's lead, accepting his selection of poems from each book and agreeing that the two of them would take their time. No schedule, no deadline.

Reflecting the creative process of balancing one's intention and drive with the gifts the Muse bestowed on them, the project proceeded with discoveries emerging at every session ... ideas and inspiration, lessons about the translation process, the poems and the poets, as well as the country and culture that produced them. Joel and Robert also gained abundant insights into their own conception and practice of poetry.

Ingmar Heytze (1970) was born and raised in Utrecht and continues to live there as a recognized and honored poet of many publications, journalist, literary organizer, musician, and performer. In 2008 he was awarded the C.C.S. Croneprijs for his entire oeuvre. In 2009 the city council of Utrecht unanimously appointed him as the first official City Poet through 2011. After that, the Utrecht Poets Guild collectively assumed the post with Ingmar as a member.

The books that supplied poems for the translation are *Het beste en de rest* (The best and the rest) from 2008, *Utrecht voor beginners & gevorderden : verzamelde Utrechtse gedichten* (Utrecht for beginners & the advanced : collected Utrecht poems) from 2015, and *Voor de liefste onbekende: bijna alle gedichten* (For the most beloved unknown: almost all the poems) from 2016.

Saskia Stehouwer (1975) was born in Alkmaar and lives in Amsterdam. She studied Dutch and English literature at the Vrije Universiteit Amsterdam and worked for over ten years as an editor and project manager at Zuid-Afrika Instituut van de Vrije Universiteit. She currently works in a natural foods store and as a life-coach. Her poem "Glimpse" reached the top twenty of the Turing National Poem Prize in 2012, while several of her poems have been published in magazines and anthologies.

Her debut collection of poetry *Wachtkamers* (Waiting rooms) was published by Uitgeverij Marmer in 2014 and was awarded the prestigious Cornelis Buddingh'-prijs in 2015. Saskia's second volume *Vrije uitloop* (Free range) was published in 2016, also by Uitgeverij Marmer.

Gedichten | Poems

Ingmar Heytze

Ik dacht ik schrijf je even
om te melden hoe het is gegaan

++++

I just thought I'd write
to tell you how it's been going

Vos Onder Ijs

Deze winter, bij het schaatsen:
vos onder ijs.
Twee glazen ogen keken op

alsof hij zo omhoog zou springen
met open bek
als het plotseling zomer werd.

Ik vlucht voor honderd boeren.
Water breekt.
Ik zwem mij langzaam dood.

Mijn laatste woorden zijn gedacht
ik kan niet meer
en spreken gaat niet hier.

Het is eenzaam. Aan deze kant.
Van het papier.
Het is zo eenzaam hier.

Fox Under Ice

This winter while skating:
fox under ice.
Two glass eyes staring

as if it were suddenly summer
and he'd jump up
with open jaw.

I flee in front of a hundred farmers.
Water breaks.
I swim myself to death slowly.

My last words get thought
I can't continue
and words don't cut it here.

It's lonely. On this side.
Of the paper.
It's so lonely here.

Voor de Liefste Onbekende

Wie van ons twee heeft de ander bedacht?
    Paul Éluard

Wat ben ik blij dat ik je nog niet ken.
Ik dank de sterren en de maan
dat iedereen die komt en gaat
de diepste sporen achterlaat, behalve jij,
dat jij mijn deuren, dicht of open,
steeds voorbijgelopen bent.

Het is maar goed dat je me niet herkent.
Kussen onder straatlantaarns
en samen dwalen door de regen,
wéér verliefd zijn, wéér verliezen,
bijna sterven van verdriet –
dat hoeft nu allemaal nog niet.

Ik ben nog niet aan ons gehecht.
Ik kijk bepaald niet naar je uit.
Neem de tijd, als je dat wilt.
Wacht een maand, een jaar,
de eeuwigheid en één seconde meer –
maar kom, voor ik mijn ogen sluit.

For the Most Beloved Unknown

Which of us two thought of the other?
    Paul Éluard

I'm so happy not to know you yet.
I thank the stars and the moon
that everyone who comes and goes
leaves the deepest traces, except you,
who has continually walked past my doors,
closed or open.

It's good that you don't recognize me.
Kissing under streetlights
and wandering together through the rain,
in love again, lost again,
almost dying of grief –
that's not quite what's needed right now.

I'm not yet attached to us.
I'm certainly not on the lookout for you.
Take your time, if you want.
Wait a month, a year,
an eternity and one second more –
but come, before I close my eyes.

Bericht aan de Reizigers

They open and close you
Then they talk like they know you
They don't know you
    Joni Mitchell

Er zit een zee in mij en dat ben ik.
Ik heb mezelf al tien jaar niet gezien.
Wanneer ik naar mij toe reis, keer ik
halverwege onverrichter zake terug.
Iemand zegt dat ik er eindelijk eens
om zou moeten huilen, maar waar
laat een zee zijn tranen? Iemand
anders is jaloers. Hij zegt: 'Jij hebt
tenminste een verhaal.' Schuim
drijft door zijn blikveld. Ik herhaal:
de zee heeft geen verhaal.

Er zit een verre stad in mij. Daar
moet ik heen. Maar alles is zo lang
geleden en misschien, als ik er ben,
loop ik wat rond, zie niets, herken
geen mens en huilt mijn heimwee
even hard. Er ligt een land in mij,
daar kon ik vroeger reizen maar het
werd te klein, het ligt in groene tegels
tussen asfaltwegen, ieder plein onder
de hemel is zo leeg, ik waai steeds
weer terug naar huis.

Attention Travelers

They open and close you
Then they talk like they know you
They don't know you
     Joni Mitchell

There is a sea in me and I am it.
I haven't seen myself for ten years.
When I travel toward myself, I return
halfway without success.
Someone says I should
just break down and cry, but where
does a sea shed its tears? Someone
else is jealous. He says, "You
at least have a story." Sea-foam
drifts through his field of vision. I repeat:
the sea has no story.

There is a distant city in me.
That's where I have to go. But everything is so
long ago and maybe, if I'm there,
I'll walk around a little, see nothing, recognize
nobody and cry really hard
from homesickness. There is a country in me,
I could have traveled there earlier but it
became too small, it's laid out in green tiles
between paved roads, each square
under the sky is so empty. Once again
I'm blown back home.

De tijd, de zee, de stad, het land,
de hemel en de pleinen zijn er
dag en nacht, ik moet eens lekker
weg in eigen hoofd maar altijd reis
ik met mezelf mee en ik ben klaar
met het gedrein: niet in de trein,
niet met de bus, alleen naar
Halverwege Onverrichter Zake
en terug – niemand kan zo groots
vergaan als ik. Er zit een zee
in mij en ik verdrink.

Time, the sea, the city, the country,
the sky and the squares are there
day and night, I need to travel well
in my own head since I'm always
with myself, so I'm through
with whining: it's not the train,
not the bus, just the going to
Halfway Without Success
and back — no one can founder as magnificently
as I can. There's a sea
in me and I'm drowning.

Aan de Bruid

If it was raining kisses he'd be the only person with an umbrella.
    Terry Pratchett

Ik dacht ik schrijf je even
om te melden hoe het is gegaan,

maar de kaart blijft ongeschreven.
Er is geen beginnen aan.

Ik leef nog steeds – een vorig leven
dat me niet is toegestaan,

ik fiets nog steeds bij je vandaan
met alle lichten tegen.

Het wordt later en ik mis je.
Je bent inkt onder mijn huid.

Het is voorjaar en het regent
en je zoekt een trouwjurk uit.

To the Bride

If it was raining kisses he'd be the only person with an umbrella.
    Terry Pratchett

I just thought I'd write
to tell you how it's been going,

but the card remains unwritten.
It's pointless.

I'm still living a past life
I'm not allowed.

I still bicycle past your place
coming up against all those red lights.

It's getting later and I miss you.
You're ink under my skin.

It's spring and it's raining
and you're picking out a wedding dress.

Wij Zorgen Ervoor

Dit wordt zo'n brief waar je spijt van krijgt.
Je voelt het al als de pen het papier raakt, dit

wordt zuivere waarheid en daar zit niemand
op te wachten. Zo'n verzameling hanenpoten,

vraag- en uitroeptekens die je haastig in een
envelop frommelt en verkeerd frankeert.

Zo'n brief die je vervolgens met een pollepel
of een ander wanhopig stuk gereedschap

weer uit de brievenbus probeert te vissen,
bij voorkeur in de regen en zonder succes.

Zo'n brief waarvoor je vloekend op de fiets
stapt om in het holst van de nacht een nieuwe

brief te gaan bezorgen: andere brief niet
openmaken, sorry voor het ongemak.

Zo'n brief waarvan je bedenkt dat dit misschien
niet afdoende is, zodat je de rest van de nacht

ten einde raad de postbode opwacht met een
onwaarschijnlijk verhaal. Zo'n sort brief dus,
over jou en mij en dat het allemaal —

We'll Take Care of It

This may be a letter you regret.
You already feel it when the pen touches the paper, this

becomes the bare truths that no one
looks for. Such a collection of scrawls,

question marks and exclamation points which you
hurriedly fumble into an envelope with incorrect postage.

A letter which you subsequently try
to fish out of the mailbox with a ladle

or another desperate kind of tool,
preferably in the rain and without success.

A letter for which you hop on your bike,
swearing, in the middle of the night, with a new

letter to deliver: the other letter
not to be opened, sorry for the trouble.

A letter which you think maybe
doesn't settle the matter, so you spend the rest of the night

desperately waiting for the postman
with your improbable story. With this kind of letter,
about you and me and all that —

Utrecht 2001

Utrecht is een grijze dame met een opgebroken hart.
Utrecht is een toverstad waar baksteen groeit tot kathedralen.
Utrecht is een pleisterplaats voor magistraten, zenuwlijders,
zakkenwassers, zakkenvullers, dromers en vandalen.

Utrecht is een knekelveld van oude sarcofagen.
Utrecht is geheime tuinen, binnenplaatsen vol seringen,
singels waar nog vogels zingen – Utrecht is de Zwaansteeg
met de zon er schuin doorheen. Utrecht is van licht en steen.

Utrecht is een stad waar je niet weg kunt en niet blijven
om er stijlvol te vergrijzen tussen kroegen, kerken en paleizen,
aan vertwijfeling ten prooi. Utrecht is een gouden kooi.

Utrecht is een plek aan de rivier waar ooit drie schepen landden,
lang begraven werkershanden palen sloegen, stenen sjouwden,
huizen bouwden, vuren brandden.

Utrecht 2001

Utrecht is a gray lady with a broken heart.
Utrecht is a magical city where brick grows into cathedrals.
Utrecht is a meeting place for judges, neurotics,
sycophants, profiteers, dreamers and vandals.

Utrecht is a graveyard of old sarcophagi.
Utrecht is secret gardens, courtyards full of lilacs,
canals where birds still sing – Utrecht is the Zwaansteeg
with its slanting sun. Utrecht is light and stone.

Utrecht is a city where you cannot leave and cannot stay,
aging there in style among pubs, churches and palaces,
prey to despair. Utrecht is a golden cage.

Utrecht is a spot on the river where three ships once landed,
where the hands of long-buried workers pounded the *palen*,
carried the stones, built the houses, lit the fires.

160

Stadgedicht aan een muur in Utrecht

> Ik stuur je dit van
> boven, deze letters
> zijn mijn ogen. Ik
> zie je vaker lopen,
> lees de briefjes op
> je telefoon. Ook dit
> bericht past in je
> hand: ik heb je lief.

160
City poem on a wall in Utrecht

> I send you this from
> above, these letters
> are my eyes. I
> see you walking more often,
> reading the messages on
> your phone. This
> one also fits in your
> hand: I love you.

Utrecht Voor Beginners
Stadgedicht aan een muur in Utrecht

Kijk niet op een jaar of wat
voor goed begrip van deze stad.
Wie op zoek wil naar het hart
kan graven tot hij is verdwenen
in een gat van twintig eeuwen.

U kunt op zoek in boeken
zwaar als kloostermoppen
of een wenteltrap beklimmen
tot het raadsel aan uw voeten ligt.
Toch geeft dit geen beter zicht.

Zoek een goede avond uit,
loop de grachten langs en kijk
hoe het licht in de huizen verdwijnt.
Leg dan uw handen op een muur.
Hier heeft de oudste steen gelijk.

Utrecht for Beginners
City poem on a wall in Utrecht

Don't look for a year or so
to get a good sense of this city.
Anyone seeking the heart of the matter
can dig until he disappears
into a hole of twenty centuries.

You can seek out books
heavy as monastery bricks
or climb a spiral staircase
until the puzzle lies at your feet.
Yet this doesn't give a better view.

Choose a good evening,
walk along the canals and look
how the light disappears in the houses.
Put your hands on a wall then.
Here the oldest stone has it right.

Stadsdichten
Stadgedicht aan een muur in Utrecht

Zolang je maar geen loflied schrijft.
Zolang je maar bereid blijft niet te zingen,
maar te fluisteren als water – murmelend
door de goten boven je hoofd, ruisend
in de buizen onder onze voeten.

Zolang je inziet dat de stad een deel
van jou is, evengoed als andersom. Zolang
je voelt dat elke stad de hartslag heeft
van jou en mij en iedereen, van
dag tot dag tot dag tot dag.

Zolang je maar begrijpt dat oude muren
oude sterren zijn: licht op leeftijd, eeuwen
onder weg. Zolang je meer geheimen kent
dan je verraadt. Zolang je altijd weg
wilt, maar nooit gaat.

City Poetry
City poem on a wall in Utrecht

As long as you don't write hymns of praise.
As long as you're prepared not to sing,
but to whisper like water — murmuring
along the gutters overhead, rustling
in the drainpipes under our feet.

As long as you realize the city's a part
of you, and vice versa. As long as
you feel each city has the heartbeat
of you and me and everyone, from
day to day to day to day.

As long as you understand that old walls
are old stars: ancient light, centuries
in the making. As long as you know
more secrets than you betray. As long as
you always want to leave, but never do.

Saskia Stehouwer

teken een boom
zodat ik kan zien waar je voeten staan
teken een boom

++++

draw a tree
so I can see where your feet are planted
draw a tree

Het Onvermogen van de Voorbijganger

+++

wat betreft de watervogels
ik beweer niet dat ik ze gezien heb
ik zeg niet dat ze zwart waren
of zwommen
misschien waren ze er
die dag wel niet

ze gooiden hun veren af
en renden weg

de vleugels
in het gras
kindersokken

The Inability of the Passerby

+++

concerning the waterbirds
I don't claim to have seen them
I'm not saying they were black
or were swimming
maybe they were not
even there that day

they threw off their feathers
and ran away

the wings
in the grass
children's socks

Bezoek

haar wijst naar het noorden
handen wapperen een bevel
naar de tas die onbereikbaar op de grond ligt
een pad dat eindigt in fluisterende auto's
een vader die discreet zijn kind het perron opduwt

ze raakt mijn schedel
vlak bij de plek
waar jij vroeg
wat ik wilde worden

niemand komt haar halen
haar stem geen partij
voor haar stuiterende armen
lichaam dat wil stijgen
boven alle nieuwbouw
boven de slechte huid
het kan geregeld worden
als de pauze lang genoeg duurt

er is geen kleingeld in dit dorp
wel vrouwen met baarden
en verregende kinderen

we halen de borrelnoten uit de vuilnisbak
en zetten ons aan tafel
kom eens langs
we zitten er nog

Visit

hair pointing north
hands waving a command
to the purse lying on the ground out of reach
a path that ends in whispering automobiles
a father discreetly pushing his child onto the train platform

she touches my skull
right by the spot
where you asked
what I wanted to become

no one comes to collect her,
her voice no match
for her flailing arms,
a body that wants to rise
above all the new building
above her old skin
it can be arranged
if one waits long enough

there's no small change in this village
there are women with beards
and rain-drenched children

we take the nuts out of the trash can
and gather around the table
come join us
we're still sitting here

Twee Kantjes

hier is de sleutel
kijk rustig rond de familie is weg
niet dat het ze niet beviel hier
maar ze waren ergens anders nodig
als u begrijpt wat ik bedoel
let op de lichtinval
het bad wordt nog gerepareerd hoor
tot zo

het huis halfvol dwalende stoelen
de zure lucht van vermoeide melk
ons kleine stuiptrekkende broertje
kijkt vreemd op vanuit zijn wieg
de moeder verrookt haar zorgen
in een asbak die alles hebben kan
we volgen het spoor van de vader
tot aan de voordeur
een kruis gekerfd naast de kruk
tot hier en niet verder

is het iets voor u mevrouw?

de ruzies op zondagmiddag
de verplichte bezoekjes
die met de tanden op elkaar
en de plooien in de broek worden uitgevoerd
als je een foto neemt van de stilte
kun je de woorden lezen die opdoemen
in een groezelig hoekje van de keuken
dit was ons terrein omdat niemand
ons iets anders wist bij te brengen
onze hoofden te stijf voor het spelletjesgevoel
de bromvliegen te nadrukkelijk aanwezig

Two Sides

here's the key
take your time looking around the family is gone
not that they didn't like it here
but they needed to be somewhere else
if you get what I mean
notice the light coming in
the bath will be repaired
be back in a minute

the house half-full of stray chairs
the sour smell of old milk
our fitful little brother
looks out curiously from his crib
the mother smokes her worries away
into an ashtray which can hold anything
we follow the path of the father
up to the front door
a cross notched next to the door handle
up to here and no further

what do you think, ma'am?

the fights on sunday afternoon
the obligatory visits
with teeth on edge
and creased pants
if you take a photo of the silence
you can read the words that loom
in a dingy corner of the kitchen
this was our space because nobody
showed us anything else
our heads too stiff for playfulness
the houseflies too strong a presence

ik strijk het gordijn in de kinderkamer glad
met de vals grijnzende kinderdieren
de hond des huizes stuift door de gang
totdat iemand op zijn staart gaat staan
gewoon omdat het kan

waar blijft het zusje?

daar staat ze met een appel in haar handen
altijd bereid tot een ordelijke vlecht
een stapje extra uit de voorraadkamer
als de anderen het maar zien
haar zomers langer door hun zwartgalligheid
haar cirkel groter telkens als zij spugen
op haar goede manieren
ze spant een draad tussen aanrecht
en kattenluik
en wacht geduldig

ons broertje peuzelt aan de klimop
en wordt bestraffend toegesproken
heimelijk wenst de moeder zich
dezelfde kaken om in het bed te zetten
haar afdruk een boodschap
te laten zijn het tandenloze zusje
een kraag aan te naaien

het is belangrijk om door de
vorige bewoners heen te kijken
uw toekomst hangt niet af van
dit geelgeschilderde muurtje
het is aan u
om er iets eigens van te maken

ik kijk naar de tekening
van een boot in mijn hand
schuif mijn ribben recht
en hijs de zeilen

in the nursery I smooth out the curtain
with the falsely-grinning baby animals
the family dog rushes through the hall
until you step on his tail
simply because you can

where is the sister?

there she stands with an apple in her hands
always ready with her braid in place
one step out of the pantry
as long as the others see her
her summers lasting longer because of their pessimism
her circle larger whenever they spit on
her good manners
she draws a string between the dresser
and cat-door
and waits patiently

our little brother munches on the ivy
and gets scolded,
secretly the mother longs for
the same jaws to set
her imprint in the bed
to leave a message sew a collar
on the toothless sister

it's important to
look beyond the previous occupants
your future does not depend on
this wall painted yellow
it's up to you
to make it your own

I look at the drawing
of a boat in my hand
slide my ribs straight
and hoist the sails

Huismeester

rechtop tussen een halve eeuw
aan sigarenbandjes en gescheiden afval
overziet hij zijn opties

twee nette pakken
aan een touwtje
boven de tafel

op dinsdag gaat hij naar de markt
koopt zijn bescheiden porties fruit
fluit een liedje voor een vrouw
die te goed weet wie ze is
op het dak prutst hij
aan een gangenstelsel

de stemmen die hem vertellen
dat hij ook kan springen

als iets de mensen niet bevalt
daalt hij af en vermaalt het
tot een gladde puree
die goed op de muren blijft zitten
die de monden vult en de lekkende buizen
onder de trap

elke avond kiest hij een huis uit om in te wonen
elke ochtend worden ze samen wakker

Caretaker

sitting upright between a half-century
of cigar bands and old rubbish
he surveys his options

two smart suits
on a string
above the table

on tuesday he goes to the market
buys his modest portions of fruit
whistles a tune for a woman
who knows too well who she is
on the roof he tinkers
with his enclave

the voices that tell him
he could also jump

if there's something the people don't like
he comes down and crushes it
into a smooth paste
that sticks to the walls
which fills the mouths and the leaky pipes under
the stairs

every evening he picks out a house to live in
every morning they wake up together

Nu

en dus zou het kunnen dat een man
in oude pekela een molendag organiseert
terwijl een vrouw in calcutta een kleed
strikt van schoenveters
de dop hoeft niet terug op de fles
want het is te koud om iets anders te doen

hier waar het bos pas op de plaats maakt
voor een onduidelijk maar agressief veld
dat zijn hek draagt als een armband

tussen de aardappelschillen
en de haastig aangeklede bruid
zit de huiskat die berekent
welk voordeel hij uit deze situatie kan halen

het is een kwestie van huid
dik genoeg om de keukendeur
's nachts open te laten
rimpels waar voorraad inpast
voor magere jaren

je hebt de herfst nodig
om de winter door te komen

Now

and so there might be a man
in oude pekela who organizes a windmill day
while a woman in calcutta makes a carpet
from shoelaces
you don't have to put the cap back on the bottle
because it's too cold to do anything else

here where the forest comes to a stop
for an unclear but aggressive field
that wears its fence like a bracelet

between the potato peelings
and the hastily dressed bride
sits the housecat who calculates
what advantage he can get from this situation

it's a matter of skin
thick enough for the kitchen door
to be left open at night
wrinkles that can keep provisions
for lean years

you need the autumn
to get through the winter

Voor

als het zwaar wordt
schrijf met potlood
draag een lichtere jas

als je je een man herinnert
beschrijf die dan
laat anders ruimte over

de reclames vallen
nauwelijks meer op
wel het kleinste scheurtje
in een nagel

dat ik niet weet
welke kleur verf hij koos
om haar rustig te houden
hoe hij soms in dezelfde stad
haar voorlas
een pantser brak

ik zal ijsjes voor je kopen
ik zal uien voor je huilen
ik zal je inmaken in
mijn kelder onder het tapijt

voor de dunne winters
voor iets voor later

ik kan het huis niet meer vinden
op de kaart die ik heb gekocht
het staat leeg
het mag niet vergeten worden

soms leg ik een hand op de muur
om te voelen of de buren thuis zijn

For

when the going gets tough
write with a pencil
wear a lighter jacket

if you remember a man
describe him then
otherwise leave the space blank

the ads are
barely noticeable
unlike the smallest crack
in a fingernail

I don't know
what color paint he chose
to keep her quiet
how sometimes in the same city
he read to her
a chink in her armor

I will buy ice cream for you
I will cry onions for you
I will preserve you in
my basement under the carpet

for the thin winters
for something for later

I cannot find the house
on the map I bought
it stands empty
it must not be forgotten

sometimes I lay a hand on the wall
to feel if the neighbors are home

Wij Sturen Niemand naar Bed

teken een vis
zodat ik kan zien wat je handen doen
teken een vis

wij leren niemand op te staan voor oude dames
wij kiezen geen scholen uit

wij kunnen eten wanneer we willen
niemand spreekt ons tegen

teken een boom
zodat ik kan zien waar je voeten staan
teken een boom

niemand zegt zijn eerste woord tegen ons
niemand zal straks lopen zoals wij
wij verzinnen onze namen op papier

teken een huis

onze tijd kijkt helder uit zijn ogen
in ons hoofd past een extra bed
onze oren spreiden hun armen

wij herijken
wij missen niet

We Send No One to Bed

draw a fish
so I can see what your hands are doing
draw a fish

we don't teach anyone to stand up for old ladies
we don't choose schools

we can eat when we want
no one tells us otherwise

draw a tree
so I can see where your feet are planted
draw a tree

no one says the first word to us
no one's going to walk like we do
we forge our names on paper

draw a house

our time has a clear look in its eyes
an extra bed fits in our head
our ears spread their arms out

we recalibrate
we don't miss

Schifting

voor wie zich een kamer zonder vloer voelt
voor wie vindt dat hij het niet koud mag hebben
voor wie op groene slippers door de zee loopt
weet dat de brandblusser gezekerd is
met een speciaal geel draadje
dat er een buurman in je straat is
die zijn kat uitlaat

weet dat het zorgvuldig bestuderen
van een lieveheersbeestje
kan uitgroeien tot een levenstaak
dat de appelboom zomaar
een opleving kan krijgen

voor wie zijn hoofd opdeelt in hokjes
zijn melk alleen rechtsom mag kloppen
zich afvraagt of het gas uit is
geloof dat een slak die je over de sloot gooit
een nieuw leven begint aan de overkant
dat een geverfd huis een ander huis wordt
dat alles een teken is

weet dat de geur van rust in elke oksel zit
dat het sluiten van de gordijnen alleen bevredigt
als er geen treinrails achter lopen

Sifting

for the one who feels like a room without a floor
for the one who thinks he should not be cold
for the one who walks by the sea in green flip-flops
know that the fire extinguisher is secured
with a special yellow wire
that there is a neighbor on your street
who walks his cat

know that the careful study
of a ladybug
can grow into a life's work
that the apple tree can suddenly
bring about a revival

for the one whose head is divided into compartments
whose milk may only be stirred clockwise
who wonders if the gas is turned off
trust that when a snail is thrown across a ditch
it begins a new life on the other side
that a house painted becomes another house
that everything is a sign

know that the odor of peace resides in every armpit
that the closing of the curtains only brings satisfaction
if there are no train tracks running behind them

Stappen in de Straat

het kind dat hier geboren wordt
weet dat het weer in het noorden onstaat
het kind dat hier geboren wordt
is toegerust voor grote daden
het kind dat hier geboren wordt
proeft of een gerecht goed bereid is
ook al kunnen zijn oma's niet koken

als er sneeuw is zal het kind
de anderen vertellen wat te doen
voor de oogst mislukken kan
zal het ingrijpen en de planten rechtop zetten
want het kind dat hier geboren is
slaat geen volle maan over

het kind dat hier geboren wordt
zal de sleutel hebben van elke deur
het zal kleine berichten hoeden
en elke middag zal het kind
kijken naar de bomen in de tuin
en elk blad dat te zien is zal het opslaan
voor de kinderen die hier geboren worden

het kind dat hier geboren wordt
voelt het verdriet van een dood dier
heeft een wit laken voor zich
kiest zelf de kleur van zijn boodschap
en weet dat brood bestaat
bij de gratie van boter

Footsteps in the Street

the child who is born here knows
that weather comes from the north
the child who is born here
is equipped for great deeds
the child who is born here
can taste whether a dish is well-prepared
even though his grandmas can't cook

if there is snow the child
will tell the others what to do
before the harvest can fail
he will intervene and stake the plants
the child who is born here
doesn't miss a full moon

the child who is born here
will have the key to every door
will care for little messages
and every afternoon the child will
look at the trees in the garden
and he will keep each leaf to be seen
for the children who are born here

the child who is born here
feels the grief of a dead animal
holds out a white sheet
he chooses the color of his message
and knows that bread exists
by the grace of butter

als het slaapt klinkt zijn moeders
stem door in zijn dromen
als het speelt voelt het
hoe jong zijn benen zijn
als het eet glijdt de warmte
van het land door zijn keel
en hoort het de muziek van de akkers

het kind dat hier geboren wordt
zal iets achterlaten
zal een bewoner zijn

when he sleeps, his mother's
voice resounds in his dreams
when he plays, he feels
how young his legs are
when he eats, the warmth
of the country slides down his throat
and he hears the music of the fields

the child born here
will leave something behind
will be at home

Essays

So much depends upon … a Dutch poet
by Robert Perry

Yes, for me, so much does depend upon a Dutch poet, or to be precise, Dutch poetry. This is my *red wheelbarrow* from the William Carlos Williams poem of that name.

I find this is the best way I can identify and embody the essence of my particular adventures in poetry—reading and writing, designing and publishing, and lately, translating Dutch poetry into my native language of American English.

It began with an assignment in my Dutch language class at the University of California at Berkeley in the early nineteen seventies—the translation of a short poem by Remco Campert … From then until now, my interest in Dutch poetry and art and all manner of things Dutch led me to establish Dutch Poet Press and choose that particular name for the imprint. With the press, I wanted to bring together in one endeavor my interests and activities in art, design, and poetry.

As with the creative process, this book of Dutch poetry in translation came about in a mode of synchronicity. It's what I enjoy calling the *lattice of coincidence*. In the act of putting something out into the world, like starting a poetry press, wonderful things often happen to one's delight and astonishment.

And so it was that Joel Katz, a fellow poet I've known for years from my local poetry group, showed up at my table at a book arts fair when my press had just published its first book. Joel came with a handful of treasures—books of Dutch poetry, a story to tell me about visiting Amsterdam and finding Dutch poems to translate into English, and questions about publishing poetry.

At that moment I could not imagine a more ideal book to design and publish for my new press.

My awe and enthusiasm joined those other raptures I've known, such as standing in front of Mondrian's *Red Cloud* or leaning against the façade of Amsterdam's ornate Central Station in a late autumn sunlight. There I took in the *Stationsplein*, the Dutch sky, and the wonder I felt on my first arrival in the Netherlands.

Relying on a *spreekwoord* that was used for the title of one of my Dutch language primers, I can say all this was *Een Goed Begin* for our translation project, as in "*Een goed begin is het halve werk*" ... "A good beginning is half the work."

++++

INSPIRATION

The Dark Room & *In Altre Parole*

When this project fell into my lap, I thought of the video I watched on *The New Yorker Online* of author Jhumpa Lahiri describing her creative process on how she wrote her novels and short stories.

In the segment, she talked about her working method—how she brought the unmanifest into form, from a dark room where there is nothing into words on the page, as if the stories were brought into the light as they gained form. She described how she shaped and refined the manuscript she had written. In draft after draft, she removed what didn't work until she arrived at the final version ready to print and send out into the world.

So it was for Joel and me in our creative project. We experienced the iterative process of transformation, of making a potentiality into an actuality, bringing what is there but unseen into the light. We explored the many possibilities that emerged in the process, choosing what we were most satisfied with and believed would ultimately stand as the completed work—in our case, the translation of poetry from Dutch into English.

The lattice of coincidence once again played in our favor just as our project was getting started. Jhumpa Lahiri published a new book *In Other Words | In Altre Parole* (Alfred A. Knopf, New York and Toronto, 2016) about her experience of living in another language—speaking, reading, and writing in Italian. She wrote the book in Italian and delegated the task of translation to another person, Ann Goldstein.

Like Lahiri with Italian, Joel and I embraced the object of our affection and attention—the Dutch language and culture through the poems of Ingmar Heytze and Saskia Stehouwer. Lahiri's commentary provided inspiring and instructive insights with abundant description and metaphor that closely reflected our own experiences.

I was right there with Lahiri when I read about the anxiety and rapture of her personal transformation when she recalls the section of Ovid's *Metamorphoses* with Daphne in Apollo's embrace, her branches for arms, bark for skin, heart beating within—the state of being in two worlds at once, drawing on what is gained, mourning what is lost.

The experience of transformation and negotiating the "otherness" of a language not one's own that Lahiri relates so eloquently in *In Other Words | In Altre Parole* led us to the title of our book *iets anders | something else*. For this and more, we are grateful.

Poets Who Translate

Along with what we learned from Lahiri about the creative process and living in a language, Joel and I benefited greatly in our translation efforts from being poets ourselves. Right from the start, we stuck to the premise that "the better the understanding, the better the translation."

In *The Art of Empathy: Celebrating Literature in Translation* published by the National Endowment of the Arts in 2014, we read that the process of translation is similar to, or can in fact be, another form of writing. We found that to be true in our experience. The author of one of the essays cautioned the poet who translates another's poetry to be careful not to write his own poem in the translation he produces. This is advice we sought to follow.

We also pursued our translations with the knowledge that "When the Muse Speaks, the poet listens and writes." We relied on the notion that poetry is a gift received both consciously and unconsciously, and is shaped and refined by the poet (and later by an editor) toward the goal of eventually sharing the creation with the world.

We were equally aware of the reservoir of inspiration, those tangible and intangible elements that are given expression through metaphor, allusion, and other means. This awareness prompted us to take into account the *denotation* and *connotation* of the text we were translating.

In doing this, we thought of *denotation* as the "prose" reading of a piece of writing or a work of art, and *connotation* as the "poetic" reading—a piece with a metaphor or vehicle leading one to grasp what is beyond ordinary understanding, to what is considered ineffable. (From *The Power of Myth*, interviews of Joseph Campbell with Bill Moyers, published by Doubleday, 1988.)

To ensure the English version of the Dutch carried the same expression or sense, we continually asked out loud "What is the *denotation* and *connotation* of this word, phrase, stanza?"

With these considerations in our translation of Ingmar's and Saskia's poetry, we made amazing and revealing discoveries about the poets, the Dutch language and culture, and the awesome capacity for what the language of poetry can express. I share these discoveries as I discuss their poetry in greater detail below.

++++

TWO POETS of the Netherlands

Our two poets live and work in the Netherlands where one views a world on a flat horizon, in which everything seen is thrown into relief and takes on greater dimension and significance. This takes place under the Dutch sky—that vast arena of Delft blue tinted with mist and mountains of shape-shifting clouds with an ever-present sense that something momentous is about to happen.

It usually does in the form of weather. In a single afternoon, it can go from cloudy to stormy, then back to peace and sunshine.

The poets were born and raised in a country of distinct elements of land, water, and sky—a jot of a republic shaped like a lion *rampant*, more man-made than God-given, where geography and history are inescapable. Whatever the era or style, artists and writers in the Netherlands are given to expression in quaint, concise essentials and telling detail, at once personal and universal, provincial and cosmopolitan, where art, philosophy, and science meet the ineffable, and where the spiritual or transcendent is present in the prosaic.

Through the translation of their poetry, Joel and I discovered how Ingmar and Saskia, each in their own way, exemplify and explore notable aspects of this ethos and sensibility.

++++

INGMAR Heytze

Above all else, Ingmar Heytze is a city poet, in his case, Utrecht, a vigorous centuries-old metropolis in the center of Holland. Being a journalist, he focuses on the here and now—the who, what, where, and when—but the poet in him takes us into the realm of the how and why. He shows us the consequences of longing and desire, the wishful, magical thinking found in the affairs of the heart.

We were not surprised to learn of his love for, and the profound influence of, contemporary songwriters. (They include Joni Mitchell, Leonard Cohen, among many others from Holland and elsewhere.) His turn of phrase and the circumstances of his protagonists show him to be a scribe of the modern songbook, at times bringing to mind Cole Porter and Lorenz Hart.

From Ingmar we learn about the traveler, even when he is in his own country or city. We learn about the observer, his encounter with his surroundings and situation.

Ingmar takes the reader from exterior to the interior. He shows how a person is transformed by where he is in the world and how he experiences it.

In "Attention Travelers" he declares "There is a sea in me and I am it." … "There is a distant city in me." … "There is a country in me." In this last phrase, he continues "… but it became too small, it's laid out in green tiles between paved roads, each square under the sky is so empty. Once again I'm blown back home."

In the four city poems in this collection, Ingmar focuses on his hometown of Utrecht. This city enables Ingmar to get to the heart of the matter, the essential verities of the Dutch metropolis, in contrast to the country's showy cultural capital of Amsterdam or the seat of its government, Den Haag. The poet captures his city and its own distinctive character most completely in "Utrecht 2001".

To geography and physical setting, the poet adds history: "Utrecht is a magical city where brick grows into cathedrals." Also there are the people—who they are and what they contributed:

> Utrecht is a spot on the river where three ships once landed, where the hands of long-buried workers pounded the *palen*, carried the stones, built the houses, lit the fires.

The city's growing modernity is not reflected in this poem or the others, as there is no mention of new architecture. However, new communication through the smartphone is present in the wall poem "160"—a new poetic form written in exactly 160 characters just like a text message. Ingmar brings delightful intimacy to that message, concluding with "This one also fits in your hand: I love you."

In his city poems Ingmar puts the reader in touch with the feel of walking the city streets in a tangible and personal way. He suggests to the reader: "Choose a good evening, walk along the canals". In another poem he declares:

> As long as you realize the city's a part
> of you, and vice versa. As long as
> you feel each city has the heartbeat
> of you and me and everyone, from
> day to day to day to day.

Ingmar puts the reader in touch, literally, with the walls and bricks of Utrecht from which wisdom is received, "As long as you understand that old walls are old stars: ancient light, centuries in the making." He invites the reader, "Put your hands on a wall then. Here the oldest stone has it right."

In other poems, Ingmar guides the reader on a tour of the human heart, the sights and sounds of unrequited love and variations on this theme. Again, this is when Ingmar is the poet's version of the astute and charming and poignant songbook lyricist. In "For the Most Beloved Unknown", Ingmar leaves the reader (and himself) on tenterhooks in the last verse, which reminds me of Hoagy Carmichael's ironic "I Get Along Without You Very Well".

> Take your time, if you want.
> Wait a month, a year,
> an eternity and one second more –
> but come, before I close my eyes.

Reading his "To the Bride" will break your heart, but never make you want to suggest to the poet that he let go and move on (well, almost never).

> I still bicycle past your place
> coming up against all those red lights.
>
> It's getting later and I miss you.
> You're ink under my skin.
>
> It's spring and it's raining
> and you're picking out a wedding dress.

Joel and I found that Ingmar's straightforward, accessible language in his depiction of city life made our job of translating his poetry easier. And his lyrical verse made it a delight.

Nevertheless it was an intriguing challenge for us to produce an English version of Ingmar's poetry which captures the extraordinary sense of empathy and charm that he brings to the everyday world of very human aspirations and fallibilities.

++++

SASKIA Stehouwer

Saskia Stehouwer is a poet of the imagination who is grounded in the curious, compelling, and often puzzling life of people and their place on earth. In fact, her namesake of *Stehouwer* speaks directly to this premise. In Dutch *stee* means "place" and is related to the words for city, *stede* or *stad*. With *houwer* her name is a form of the historically significant title of *stadhouder*, the regents or incumbents who represented Dutch cities. The verb *houden* can mean "to hold" "to keep" or "to love".

For Saskia, that place is The Netherlands. Her poems belong to the present day, but they are imbued with a cultural ethos connected to history and geography. Her works possess traditional Dutch attributes that appear in a modern context by a poet living in the twenty-first century.

Consider her poem "Footsteps in the street" about a magical child with an intuitive understanding of the workings of the earth:

> the child who is born here knows
> that weather comes from the north
> the child who is born here
> is equipped for great deeds

or the "Caretaker" about a very different sort of person:

> sitting upright between a half-century
> of cigar bands and old rubbish
> he surveys his options
>
> two smart suits
> on a string
> above the table

In her poem "Now" she presents the Dutch landscape in human terms:

> here where the forest comes to a stop

> for an unclear but aggressive field
> that wears its fence like a bracelet

Spreekwoord

The most prevalent and eloquent of these cultural attributes present in Saskia's work is the *spreekwoord*, a tradition of offering a particular idea or reflection summarized in a deceptively simple saying that speaks volumes.

In the Netherlands, folk sayings and passages from the Old and New Testament, particularly the Gospels and the books of Psalms and Proverbs, found their way into the prints and emblems of Jacob Cats (1577-1660) and even on kitchen and living room tiles.

As Saskia told us, she sometimes invents her own aphorisms, as in the poem "Now":

> you need the autumn
> to get through the winter

or in "Footsteps in the street":

> he chooses the color of his message
> and knows that bread exists
> by the grace of butter

The latter example sounds like an *ars poetica*, a statement on the nature of her art. At the same time, it sounds like a proverb in which the poet elevates the prosaic bread and butter into a life lesson. Here we find the Dutch trait of employing quaint, concise essentials with telling detail, at once personal and universal.

Saskia goes even further by incorporating the *spreekwoord* form in the style and expression of her verse. It's natural for her to concentrate meaning in discrete, succinct bits of text—a phrase, a line, or a stanza, as in "We send no one to bed":

> draw a tree
> so I can see where your feet are planted
> draw a tree

or even when the scene is surreal and the meaning is enigmatic, as in "Two sides":

> if you take a photo of the silence
> you can read the words that loom
> in a dingy corner of the kitchen

The Art of Painting

The central theme of Saskia's poetic vision—the experience of place—reflects another aspect of Dutch culture which I call *The Art of Painting*, the title of one of Jan Vermeer's most famous works. It is considered to be his own *ars poetica*.

This is to say, Saskia the poet is a painter in words. Performing *The Art of Painting* in her poetry, she depicts in written and spoken language her native land, her place in the world, her *Stee*.

Her poems contain vivid imagery with potent symbols or foci of meaning conveyed through descriptive metaphor and allusion. In this way, Saskia's poetry is a modern-day exemplar of what art historian Svetlana Alpers elucidates in her landmark book *The Art of Describing: Dutch Art in the Seventeenth Century* (University of Chicago Press, 1983). Alpers asserts that the fields of science and philosophy had a profound impact on the visual arts in the Netherlands of the sixteen hundreds.

This influence is reflected in a shared interest in keen observation and clarity of vision with the premise that what is experienced and felt derives primarily from the visual, what is seen.

Saskia has inherited this tradition in the way she renders the people, places, and things of her poetry with the eye of such a painter. So much of her poetry is about putting the observable into a poetic dimension.

Consider her poem "The inability of the passerby", with its amazingly concise description of a particular scene. As we read through the poem, we join her as the observer of this scene of precise and vivid detail that is brought into our direct and immediate awareness:

> concerning the waterbirds
> I don't claim to have seen them
> I'm not saying they were black
> or were swimming
> maybe they were not
> even there that day
>
> they threw off their feathers
> and ran away
>
> the wings
> in the grass
> children's socks

While Saskia depicts an exterior scene with an enigmatic quality, her poem is reminiscent of looking at an interior by Jan Vermeer in which the viewer of the painting is invited to become the observer of a woman in profile reading a letter in front of a window.

Saskia's poetry is also reminiscent of seventeenth century Dutch still life painting by artists such as Jan Davidzn. de Heem. These painters place their subjects in shallow space close to the picture plane and slant the table top slightly forward toward the viewer for closer inspection.

In her poetry, Saskia renders her vivid imagery with a similar clarity of vision and the sense of bringing what is depicted closer to the mind's eye of the reader.

The American poet Mark Doty in his book *Still Life with Oysters and Lemon* (Beacon Press, Boston, 2001) guides us through his experience of taking in a de Heem painting of that name housed in the Metropolitan Musuem of Art in New York.

Doty shows us how the viewer becomes enraptured by the visual splendor of this Dutch still life painting. This experince reminds me of the way the reader of a poem by Saskia can become similarly transformed.

Here is a representative sampling of various lines and verses in which we experience the evocative and illuminating sense of the visual in Saskia's poetry.

From "Visit":

> hair pointing north
> hands waving a command
> to the purse ...

From "Now":

> between the potato peelings
> and the hastily dressed bride
> sits the housecat who calculates
> what advantage he can get from this situation

++++

In her visual poems of telling detail as commentary on the human condition, Saskia shares a sensibility with the contemporary Dutch artist Co Westerik, born in 1924. A stanza from her poem "For" reminded me of his seemingly monumental paintings of detailed close-ups of a finger being cut by a blade of grass:

> the ads are
> barely noticeable
> unlike the smallest crack
> in a fingernail

With a similar irony and wit, Saskia's poetry depicts people with a style of living based on compromise who continually strive to adjust to their circumstances in which something untoward usually happens.

In Saskia's poem "Caretaker", the protagonist's life is presented with starkly compromising options and the illusion that he can control his world:

> on tuesday he goes to the market
> buys his modest portions of fruit
> whistles a tune for a woman
> who knows too well who she is
>
> on the roof he tinkers
> with his enclave
>
> the voices that tell him
> he could also jump

In her poem "We send no one to bed", Saskia offers an instance in which personal choice is given a positive cast of mind and outcome. In successive verses, she provides lucid, expressive assertions like "our time has a clear look in its eyes" and concludes with this powerful stanza:

> we recalibrate
> we don't miss

++++

Yes, so much depends upon … a Dutch Poet … like Ingmar Heytze and Saskia Stehouwer who explore where and how we live with our surroundings and the people we encounter there.

With our experience of translating these poets, my original notion of the Dutch ethos and sensibility has been strengthened and extended into a new realm of understanding and rapture as vast and portentous as that awesome Dutch sky that captured my attention when I first set foot in Holland on the *Stationsplein* of Amsterdam.

The *iets anders* | *something else* of Language
by Joel Thomas Katz

The truth is I love language. I should have a t-shirt or a bumper sticker made that says "I ♥ Language". This sums up my life of learning languages in one form or another—Hebrew, Russian, French, and Dutch. This also includes studying linguistics, working as a computer programmer, playing music, and in recent years, practicing the art of poetry and translation.

Why is this so? Our translation project has made me realize, more than ever before, that it's the *iets anders | something else* of language which I enjoy so much.

Along with my delight in the *presence of pattern*—the rhythm and sequencing, the design of language—the other element I find enriching and inspiring is the *pursuit of affinity*. When I recognize something familiar in what I have not encountered before, I immediately want to understand more. I want to educate myself and practice what I've learned.

What draws me in and sustains me is my ongoing encounter with the *something else* that language provides. For poetry in particular, the *something else* is expressed in the way a poet uses language through techniques like metaphor, allusion, and other means. These take the reader (or listener) from ordinary understanding into the realm of the extraordinary and ineffable.

These notions have led me to live in a language, analyze how it is used, and employ language to interpret and create. I take pleasure in the greater gifts that language offers—not just as a medium of communication, but also as a vehicle for beauty and artistic expression in forms such as music and poetry. Through this translation project, I've learned what led me to become a poet and translator of poetry.

Languages

In my lifelong exploration of this *something else*, I've delved into several languages.

Hebrew As a young boy, I encountered Hebrew in the synagogue and at home for various religious rituals. It intrigued me that one reads Hebrew from right-to-left, so that the beginning of a Hebrew book corresponds to the end of an English book. In addition, Hebrew words are written as a series of consonants, with the vowel sounds being merely dots and lines placed either under or over those consonants. All instances of *something else*.

Russian With *Sputnik* and Khrushchev banging his shoe on the lectern at the UN, Russia and all things Russian were on everybody's mind in the sixties, including mine. I found the paperback *Russian Through Pictures*, which began with a creative approach to learning the Cyrillic (Russian) alphabet. I took it for granted that certain familiar-looking letters had either the same or different pronunciation as the corresponding English letter, or that there were strange new letters which had no corresponding ones in English. I enjoyed that I could now write the name Khrushchev just as he would write it in his language.

French By age 17, my five years of studying French in junior high and high school enabled me to visit the Expo '67 World's Fair in Montreal and bypass the long lines of English-speaking tourists. I took delight in understanding more of the French-led tours than I would have imagined, as well as being able to give directions in French to visitors.

Linguistics

My interest in experiencing the various textures of the *something else* of language led me to enroll in the Graduate Program in Linguistics at Stanford University in the early nineteen seventies. Plunging into phonetics, phonology, syntax, and semantics with gusto, I noticed that two particular questions continued to capture my attention:

> What strategies do people use to acquire an additional language alongside their native one, especially young children thrown into a new-language situation without any formal instruction?

> What patterns emerge as the children gain increasing mastery over their new language?

My research involved following two six-year-old Israeli children at Stanford playing with an American friend. To what extent did their native Hebrew interfere with the untutored English they were picking up? Or were their initially "ungrammatical" English utterances evidence of some individual perceptual strategies? I was using a computer-based statistical program to analyze my research findings.

Eventually the computer programs became more interesting than the data I was analyzing, and I made a career shift to computer programming. Now it was *computer* languages that I learned, and spent the next thirty years engaged in a new kind of *something else*, translating business processes into a code the computer could understand.

Music and Poetry

My childhood was filled with classical music, both at home, such as music on the radio and shelves of albums, and outside the home by going to weekend classical concerts at the nearby Montclair Art Museum.

After attending various concerts, I decided I wanted to play the violin. My violin lessons included memorizing longer and more complex pieces. Instead of trying to remember an increasingly longer string of notes, I began to hear themes, sub-themes, counter-melodies, and sections.

I found that the hierarchical chunks of musical ideas fit together into a single movement or an entire piece. By sensing how the parts related to the whole, I learned each piece of music intuitively through the human impulse to look for patterns.

That impulse led to my interest in poetry, which began during high school and college. With poetry, I swam in a captivating sea of rhythm, rhyme, sound patterns, line enjambment, etc. This inspired me to take literature courses about poetry as well as poetry-writing workshops. Indeed, those musical and poetic impulses coalesced into my exploring musicality in my own poetry.

This pursuit led me to a growing interest in translating non-English-language poetry, which involved travel to Israel and eventually the Netherlands.

Israel

During a trip to Israel in 1993, I stopped at a café where the Israeli poet Yehuda Amichai frequently recited his work. The café had a small shelf of books in Hebrew for sale, and I looked for the slimmest book of contemporary poems I could find. I found one by poet Rafi Weichert to take back with me to California, thinking it would be nice one day to read and understand his poetry in its original language.

Years later I decided to translate some of the poems into English and found a native Hebrew speaker in San Jose. After several sessions, we managed to translate about twenty of Weichert's poems. This experience inspired me to look for other opportunities to translate poetry.

The Netherlands

In preparation for a vacation to Holland in 2013, I began to teach myself Dutch by listening to *Learn Dutch* by the Pimsleur Language Programs over and over again. Once I arrived, I found myself in a large bookstore in Amstelveen where I asked in my elementary Dutch for the poetry section. I returned to California with the slimmest book I could find, which was *Avond Malen* (Evening Meals) by Tuvit Shlomi. With the help of a local Dutch women, I translated around twenty poems. This made me want to translate more poetry.

Before my second trip to the Netherlands in 2015, I bolstered my Dutch with another healthy dose of Pimsleur. On this visit, I discovered Perdu, the all-poetry bookstore on the Kloveniersburgwal in Amsterdam. It was there I found the books by Ingmar Heytze and Saskia Stehouwer that led to our *iets anders | something else* project.

Back in California I entered a new phase in my lifelong exploration of the *something else* of language. I took a selection of nine poems each from Ingmar and Saskia and began to translate them into English. I enlisted Robert Perry, a fellow poet from our local poetry group the Waverley Writers in Palo Alto, to help me with the translations and the publication of this book. Combining his study of Dutch language, art, and poetry with his endeavors in book design, Robert had recently launched his own imprint Dutch Poet Press. Along with becoming a co-translator, he served as the designer and publisher of our book through his press.

++++

About TRANSLATION

The Challenge of Understanding the *Something Else* of Language

The famous Italian saying *"traduttore – traditore"* (translator – traitor) serves to chasten anyone brave enough to attempt translation. It arose when Italians were displeased by French renderings of their beloved Dante, which the Italians felt had betrayed either the beauty or accuracy of the original.

So how does one go about grappling with the *something else* of language?

One reasonable approach is to recognize that certain aspects of one language are more difficult to convey in another language. The sounds and rhythms as well as the tone and register of one language may operate differently in the other language.

Another consideration is literalness: due to lexical and grammatical differences between the two languages, the original poem's phrasing and syntax may need to be rearranged in the translation. There is also the matter of how to render idioms into English.

To meet this complex of challenges, our task was to discover the best ways to capture the fullest sense of each poem. To achieve that, Robert and I found value in three specific areas: our particular approach to collaboration, our seeking advice from an expert in the Dutch language as well as the poets themselves, and our following what we called the "Alita Rule" that made certain we always referred back to the original text.

++++

OUR PROJECT

Chavruta: the Benefits of Collaboration

The hallmark of these Dutch-to-English translations of poetry is the collaborative approach we took. Our working method has a name in Hebrew—*Chavruta* ("chav-ROOT-ah": "ch" like the German *Bach* or Scottish *loch*): the mode of studying the Talmud and other writings in pairs.

Two study partners with inherently different backgrounds and sensibilities sit together, reading and vigorously discussing with each other in order to arrive at a more thorough, in-depth understanding of the chosen text. The term *Chavruta* derives from the Hebrew word *chaver* (cha-VAIR), which means friend or partner.

This method is based on the simple idea that "two heads are better than one".

These *Chavruta*-style sessions took place weekly and lasted several hours. Typically, we did as many as ten English versions of a poem until the two of us felt we had taken the translation as far as we could, short of consulting with the poets.

With constant discussion and argument between us, a continual back and forth, we dedicated ourselves to finding the right word and phrase, striving for the proper sense and meaning of each particular and the whole of the poem. We kept at it until we were both satisfied.

When considering what makes for a "satisfying" translation, Robert and I repeatedly asked each other the following questions. These served as helpful benchmarks for our translations.

- Can the translation stand on its own as a poem in English? Does the English version flow smoothly, or sound lumpy and betray the fact that it's an imperfect replica of a poem from another language?

- Since the syntax of Dutch and English differ in important ways, when is it necessary to restructure the Dutch original in the English translation?

- Does the tone or register of the original poem come across in the English translation? Are sections of the original poem notably different, such as sounding off-handed, meditative, pedantic, or ironic?

- How successfully have we conveyed Dutch idioms in English, especially when there's no obvious corresponding idiom?

In the many months spent together communing with the poems and exploring their inner workings, we learned how to read each poet's work much better. Our collaborative approach helped to sharpen and refine our evolving insights.

Throughout the process, we maintained informal rules of engagement that prescribed absolute candor and permission to question oneself and the other person as assiduously as we felt was necessary to bring any particular point to satisfaction, with the understanding this would be something to ask the poets about.

We concurred that perfection or an ideal equivalent in English was not going to be possible to attain in some, if not most, cases. Nonetheless, we agreed to make a thorough and concerted effort toward that end.

As we discovered, the benefits of our *Chavruta*-style approach to translation were tremendous. (And we're still on speaking terms.)

In the section below called *Chavruta in Action*, I provide two examples of our working method, drawn from the translation of a work from each poet.

Translation in Three Stages

The first stage consisted of our translations with observations and commentary, as well as the questions that emerged from our spirited *Chavruta* collaboration. In the next stage we benefited from review and comment from a native or expert in the Dutch language, then we ultimately received feedback from the two poets, Ingmar and Saskia.

For our part we wanted to bring the translations as far as we could before consulting with our poets. With relative ease, we found a Dutch language expert willing to take on the task of review and comment. At the Napa Valley Writers Conference, I met the fiction writer Karen Kao, an American living and working in Amsterdam. Karen turned out to have an amazing fluency and a writer's way with the Dutch language, not to mention a willingness and generosity to delve into the texts thoroughly with a keen eye for word choice and meaning. We are grateful for her contribution to our project.

Robert and I homed in on Karen's suggestions and refined the translations as much as we could. We found ourselves inundated with a vast paper trail of notations, scribbles, and cross-outs with all manner of variations and options. We decided to give Ingmar and Saskia a clean, pristine copy of our best efforts—no word options, alternative texts, or annotations.

At this point we were letting the poems in English stand and speak on their own. We kept our commentary and questions to ourselves so that Ingmar and Saskia could focus and reflect only on their poems in English as they would ultimately be presented in our book.

When we received their detailed replies, we absorbed and discussed them, once again going into *Chavruta* mode. Then we brought all of our thoughts and questions together and shared them with the poets.

As it turns out, the poets were pleased with our efforts. They were happy to have their poems receive such close attention and care. They were delighted to discover new dimensions in their poems and learn something more about their own work.

It was marvelous for us to gain insight into their intentions, useful for a more precise translation and a richer understanding of their poetry. On top of that, we learned so much about Ingmar and Saskia, as well as the Dutch ethos and sensibility that resonate throughout their work.

The Alita Rule

Robert and I are grateful for what we call the Alita Rule, a cautionary reminder to pay attention to the original text as written by the poets.

Early in the project, Robert shared a story about his son's piano teacher, Alita. She is a wonderfully demonstrative, affectionate Russian woman with a sincere mission to inculcate the rigors of proper music-making in her young charges. Prone to play a piece from memory and enhance what he learned and felt, Robert's son Joe was admonished by Alita. She told him to look at the musical score and play exactly what was written. Hence, the Alita Rule.

As Robert and I pursued our collaboration, we noticed a tendency to stray from the text in front of us. We often translated a passage in ways that extended the text beyond what was originally present in the Dutch.

It is sometimes necessary and often valuable to use more words in English to capture what's written or said in Dutch, as with an idiom or a well-turned concise phrase. A terse phrase or sentence is quite common in Dutch.

It was a useful exercise to explore various possible phrasings in English, giving us a variety of choices to consider and discuss in order to land on what we thought worked best.

Nevertheless it was important, if not essential, to remind ourselves to refer back to the original text in Dutch. So we invoked the Alita Rule often and found ourselves asking:

What is the poet saying here? ... What is his or her intention? ... What is the construction and flow of the text? ... What does it look and sound like?

++++

CHAVRUTA IN ACTION: Two Examples

Saskia Stehouwer—*"Gangenstelsel"* & *"Prutsen"*

One example of our *Chavruta* approach to translation comes from Saskia's poem *"Huismeester"* ("Caretaker"). The caretaker in this poem is responsible for maintaining a multi-floor building for various residents. Here is the relevant passage in Dutch and our final version in English (emphasis ours):

> op dinsdag gaat hij naar de markt
> koopt zijn bescheiden porties fruit
> fluit een liedje voor een vrouw
> die te goed weet wie ze is
> op het dak **prutst** hij
> aan een **gangenstelsel**
>
> . . .
>
> als iets de mensen niet bevalt
> daalt hij af . . .
>
> ++++
>
> on tuesday he goes to the market
> buys his modest portions of fruit
> whistles a tune for a woman
> who know too well who she is

> on the roof he ***tinkers***
> with his ***enclave***
> . . .
>
> if there's something the people don't like
> he comes down . . .

In other contexts, *gangenstelsel* is a corridor or passageway, as in a castle or a sewer, but in this poem, it is on the rooftop of an ordinary building. Our Dutch-language expert Karen Kao suggested that *gangenstelsel* is a maze on the roof, perhaps containing the utilities or controls of the building. Saskia told us that maze or labyrinth sounds too much like a fairy-tale or an Indiana Jones adventure movie.

Robert and I then asked the question: what actually happens in this *gangenstelsel*?

We agreed that to answer our question, we first needed to understand the operative verb in this stanza, *prutsen*. For Saskia, the word meant tweaking or tinkering. We also considered "putter" and "futz," based on the poet's mentioning the awkwardness of this caretaker fellow. She added that whatever he does up there, it is some kind of hobby or obsession, as in a basement or garage workshop, or something like working on a bomb shelter. She expressed a preference for "tweak," implying a nerd or techie.

We let the subject rest for a little while, then Robert suggested what the caretaker has is his "man-cave"—what one might call his "enclave": the designated area where he does his thing, or a bounded area enclosed in a larger area, such as the Vatican within the city of Rome.

We came to the conclusion that "enclave" is the central metaphor of this poem. The caretaker tinkers in his enclave within the building as he cares for its occupants. The *gangenstelsel* is the nexus of his caretaking, just as the Vatican has historically served as the center of Christendom.

With this understanding, we reviewed our options for *prutsen*. We selected "tinkers" because it felt like the right word to go with "enclave". To confirm this to our mutual satisfaction, we had to tackle the question of how the Dutch preposition "aan" should be rendered in English to go with "tinkers" and "enclave." I suggested that the phrase in question *"op het dak prutst hij / aan een gangenstelsel"* should be translated "on the rooftop he tinkers / **with** his enclave" rather than "… tinkers / **in** his enclave". The phrase "**with** his enclave" conveys the notion that the tinkering would include the enclave itself, not merely what it contains.

Our choice underscored the caretaker's attachment to his rooftop enclave as a special place and helped to illuminate the meaning of tinkering as an ongoing, never-ending project.

Ingmar Heytze—Contrast & Nuance

Another example of our *Chavruta* approach comes from Ingmar Heytze's poem *"Aan de bruid"* ("To the bride"). Here is the poem in Dutch and our final English version, with key passages highlighted to indicate what prompted our lively exchange of questions and ideas:

> *Aan de bruid*
>
> Ik dacht ik schrijf je even
> om te melden hoe het is gegaan,
>
> maar de kaart blijft ongeschreven.
> **Er is geen beginnen aan.**
>
> Ik leef nog steeds – een vorig leven
> dat me niet is toegestaan,

ik fiets nog steeds **bij je vandaan**
met alle lichten **tegen**.

Het wordt later en ik mis je.
Je bent inkt onder mijn huid.

Het is voorjaar en het regent
en je zoekt een trouwjurk uit.

++++

To the bride

I just thought I'd write
to tell you how it's been going,

but the card remains unwritten.
It's pointless.

I'm still living a past life
I'm not allowed.

I still bicycle **past your place
coming up against all those red lights**.

It's getting later and I miss you.
You're ink under my skin.

It's spring and it's raining
and you're picking out a wedding dress.

In the second line of the poem's second stanza, we questioned whether we should translate the intent (connotation) rather than the literal meaning (denotation). The phrase "*Er is geen beginnen aan*" literally means "There is no start (beginning) to it." However, our Dutch language expert Karen Kao felt that the phrase conveyed 'there's no point in starting; the task is pointless'. Robert and I decided on "It's pointless," a solution whose succinctness mirrors the short and direct tone of the poem as a whole.

The greatest amount of discussion took place over two phrases in the fourth stanza: "*bij je vandaan*" and "*met alle lichten tegen*". We initially considered "I still bicycle by your place." The literal meaning of *bij je* is "by you," meaning "by (or at) your place (or house)." But as Karen Kao pointed out, the preposition *vandaan* means "away" in the sense of "away from": the speaker is actually biking away from (or getting away from) wherever the other person is.

Karen also saved us from a misstep in the English. While the Dutch word *tegen* means "against, opposite, opposed," the entire phrase *lichten tegen* refers to red traffic lights. Robert and I modified our initial translation to:

> I still bicycle past your place
> with all the traffic lights turning red

I then suggested it might be useful to somehow incorporate the literal "oppositional" notion of *tegen*. Within the poem, those red lights serve to impede the speaker from smoothly bicycling past (away from) his former lover's place. This led to the phrasing:

> I still bicycle past your place
> coming up against all those red lights

We were also pleased that independent of the Dutch original, our English version was able to convey two senses of the word *past*: "I'm still living a past life" and "I still bicycle past your place".

++++

INVITATION TO UNDERSTANDING

These examples from the poems of Ingmar and Saskia show the extraordinary benefits of our *Chavruta* approach to translation—discoveries about the Dutch language and its cultural ethos.

On top of that, contrary to the Italian sentiment of *"traduttore – traditore"* (translator – traitor), our project showed us that translation offers an encouraging and necessary invitation to understanding human expression in poetry. That is to say, an invitation to a deeper understanding of ourselves.

Translation Notes

Heytze, "Utrecht 2001"

De Zwaansteeg (Swan Lane): a narrow lane connecting two larger streets in Utrecht.

"pounded the *palen*" refers to the long thick vertical poles which are sunk into the ground to support the building above, especially when the ground is near water. Older houses along canals are supported this way, as well as modern-day Amsterdam's main train station *Centraal Station*, which sits on 9000 such *palen*.

Heytze, "160" "Utrecht voor beginners" "Stadsdichten"

These are city-poems (*stadsgedichten*) which appear in large letters on the walls of buildings or on the stonework along a canal.

The title "160" refers to a poetic form derived from the layout of the smartphone where a typical screen-page allows for 160 characters. The form's requirement is to convey a message in exactly 160 characters including spaces and punctuation.

In Heyzte's poem "*Stadsdichten*", compare the placing of hands on the stones to the ending of Stehouwer's poem "*Voor*":

> sometimes I lay a hand on the wall
> to feel if the neighbors are home

Stehouwer, "Het onvermogen van de voorbijganger"

This is the subtitle of the first section of *Wachtkamers*. The poem itself serves as an untitled epigraph to that section.

"*onvermogen*" [on + vermogen]: "inability" in the broadest sense. Other possible and more specialized meanings are: inadequacy, powerlessness, incapacity, incapability.

Stehouwer, "Bezoek"
"borrelnoten": nuts that accompany glasses of liquor or beer, commonly served in Dutch bars.

Stehouwer, "Twee kantjes"
Saskia has told us that she mis-remembered a Dutch idiom in this poem. It should be "sewing an ear (*een oor aan te naaien*)" and not "sewing a collar (*een kraag aan te naaien*)". The intended idiom conveys that someone is making a fool of someone else. In this poem, the mother is making a fool of the sister because according to Saskia, the sister is "always so prim and well-behaved and secretly, the mother cannot stand her."

The idiom stems from the dubious practice years ago of having students in Dutch schools walk around with donkey ears attached to their heads to punish them for being "dumb".

Stehouwer, "Nu"
Oude Pekela is a small town in northeast Netherlands, which the poet uses to represent a typical Dutch village.

The final two lines of the poem are an example of the poet inventing her own *spreekwoord*, a proverb or adage that is a statement of profound importance expressed in an apparently simple saying.

Stehouwer, "Wij sturen niemand naar bed"
The Dutch has sound-play which we have not reproduced in the English: *"teken"* (to draw or sketch) versus *"tegen"* (against, opposite, opposed).

"No one says their first word to us." Saskia characterized the sentiment in this way: "since we will never be parents, no child will utter their first phrase in our presence."

Stehouwer, "Schifting"
"*Schifting*": a separating or partitioning. "*Schiften*": to sort, winnow, screen.

Stehouwer, "Twee kantjes" "Huismeester" "Nu"
In these poems, Saskia puts proper names in lowercase, consistent with the style of her poetry as found in the selection of this book. In the English translations, we decided to retain the lowercase treatment to reflect this practice.

Places — Oude Pekela, Calcutta
Days of the Week — Sunday, Tuesday
Special Event — Windmill Day

Colophon

Type for Display: Didot

Type for Text: Avenir Next

Cover & Interior Design: Robert Perry, Dutch Poet Press

Production & Distribution: IngramSpark

++++

When Joel and I chose the title of our book, the cover design quickly followed. I instantly fell in love with the idea of using only type. That's because my love of the Dutch language came from the typographic design I encountered everywhere I went in the Netherlands—the *Nederlandse Spoorwegen* (Dutch Railways), postage stamps, the money, and the telephone book, to name a few. In addition to that, the subject of this book is about language.

The colors I chose for the design are a variation of the orange and blue of Dutch Poet Press, reflecting the intention of the press to publish Dutch poetry in English. And in the spirit of the *lattice of coincidence*, when Saskia saw the cover design, she asked me if I had been thinking of the old version of the Dutch flag when the tricolor was blue, orange, and white. I had not, and that makes it all the more enjoyable.

www.ingramcontent.com/pod-product-compliance
Lightning Source LLC
Chambersburg PA
CBHW042100290426
44113CB00005B/108